SONALI BHATTACHARYYA

Sonali Bhattacharyya is an award-winning playwright and screenwriter (Sonia Friedman Production Award and Theatre Uncut Political Playwriting Award for *Chasing Hares*) whose credits include *Megaball* (National Theatre Learning), *Slummers* (Cardboard Citizens/Bunker Theatre), *The Invisible Boy* (Kiln Theatre) and *2066* (Almeida Participation). She is a graduate of the Royal Court Writers' Group, the Old Vic 12 and Donmar Warehouse's Future Forms Programme, and is former writer-in-residence at the Orange Tree Theatre and National Theatre Studio. She's currently under commission to Kiln Theatre, the Almeida and Fifth Word. She's from Leicester and lives in North East London.

www.sonaliwrites.com

Other Titles in this Series

Sonali Bhattacharyya

TWO BILLION BEATS

NICK HERN BOOKS

London

www.nickhernbooks.co.uk

A Nick Hern Book

Two Billion Beats first published in Great Britain in 2022 as a paperback original by Nick Hern Books Limited, The Glasshouse, 49a Goldhawk Road, London W12 8QP

An earlier version of *Two Billion Beats* was published by Nick Hern Books in 2021 in the volume *Inside/Outside: Six Short Plays*

Extract from *Sylvia Pankhurst: Natural Born Rebel* by Rachel Holmes © Rachel Holmes 2020, Bloomsbury Publishing Plc.

Cover photograph of Anoushka Chadha and Safiyya Ingar by Alex Brenner

Designed and typeset by Nick Hern Books, London
Printed in Great Britain by Mimeo Ltd, Huntingdon, Cambridgeshire PE29 6XX

A CIP catalogue record for this book is available from the British Library

ISBN   978 1 83904 072 6

Two Billion Beats was first performed at the Orange Tree Theatre, Richmond, on 5 February 2022, with the following cast:

BETTINA	Anoushka Chadha
ASHA	Safiyya Ingar

Director	Nimmo Ismail
Designer	Debbie Duru
Lighting Designer	Alex Fernandes
Sound Designer	Tingying Dong
Movement Director	Chi-San Howard
Associate Movement Director	Tian Brown-Sampson
Voice Coach	Emma Woodvine
Casting Director	Christopher Worrall
Company Stage Manager	Jenny Skivens
Deputy Stage Manager	Lara Mattison
Assistant Stage Manager	Nicole Scott
Production Manager	Stuart Burgess
Technical Manager	Lisa Hood

An earlier version of the play was first livestreamed in the Orange Tree Theatre's *Inside/Outside* season on 15 April 2021, directed by Georgia Green.

Acknowledgements

Thank you to: Paul Miller and Guy Jones for all their support, Louisa Neuberger and Rachel Holmes for their help and insights, Manju and Dilip for their encouragement and belief, and Paul, Leela and Akash for being the best of the best of the besties.

S.B.

'I thought it was only fools who were afraid of words.'

B. R. Ambedkar

Characters

ASHA, *seventeen*
BETTINA, *fifteen*

This text went to press before the end of rehearsals and so may differ slightly from the play as performed.

Scene One

ASHA, *seventeen, British Asian, empathetic rebel, reads a book in the corridor outside the sixth-form common room at her school, headphones in. The sound of an after-school club in the hall nearby can be heard faintly (basketball or something similar). ASHA's sister,* BETTINA, *fifteen, a quiet daydreamer prone to flights of fancy, also in school uniform, enters.*

BETTINA. You waiting for someone?

ASHA. What?

BETTINA. You waiting for someone?

> ASHA *turns down the volume on her phone with exaggerated annoyance.*

ASHA. No.

BETTINA. What you doing, then?

ASHA (*of her book*). What's it look like?

BETTINA. You can read at home.

ASHA. You can be an annoying little shit at home.

BETTINA. If we go now we can get the bus together.

ASHA. I'm alright, thanks.

> BETTINA *slings down her bag and gets comfortable.*

What're you doing?

BETTINA. I'll wait 'til you're done.

ASHA. Why?

BETTINA. ...Forgotten my keys.

> ASHA *roots around in her bag and produces her keys, handing them to* BETTINA.

Not taking yours.

ASHA. Why not?

BETTINA. What if I lose them?

ASHA. Then I'll kill you.

BETTINA. Exactly. Who needs that sort of pressure?

BETTINA *gives* ASHA *back her keys.*

ASHA. If you're going to hang around, find somewhere else to sit.

BETTINA. Why?

ASHA. You're putting me off.

BETTINA. I'm not doing anything.

ASHA. Exactly. It's weird, you just sitting there.

BETTINA. Let's go then?

ASHA. *No.*

BETTINA *just shrugs and makes herself comfortable.*

(*Direct address.*) Basketball club finishes at five-thirty and the caretaker'll be here to close up, so that's when I have to head off. But I'm going to take my time walking home. Don't want to get in any earlier than six-thirty. Mum will have left for work by then. She hasn't spoken to me since I handed in my essay. Not when I knock to see if it's her in the bathroom, ask her to pass me the remote, check if she wants a cup of tea… Nothing. God knows how long she's going to keep it up.

BETTINA. What did you get on your essay?

ASHA. What do you care?

BETTINA. Just taking an interest, jeez.

ASHA *takes her headphones out for a moment to recount recent events to the audience.*

ASHA (*direct address*). You start with something surprising, something clickbaity. Mrs L loves that shit. She calls it 'opening with a flourish'. *Gandhi didn't use his fists, but he was still a fighter.* Round one! In the blue corner, we have…

Gandhiji! The unlikely featherweight looking to take on the growling, spitting bulldog of the British Empire. Gandhi lands the first blow – killer quote from me, I've done my research. '*In a gentle way, you can shake the world.*' Pow. Then another one: '*Whenever you are confronted with an opponent, conquer him with love.*' Bam.

But when considering 'Can the pen be mightier than the sword?' – keep dragging it back to the essay question. *It's important to remember Gandhi didn't just write about his ideas, he saw them through in his own life. He wrote about fasting as a tool of resistance, because it's one he used, against the British. Eighteen times! The longest he fasted was twenty-one days. Fasting was Gandhi's favourite non-violent weapon, and sometimes he used it against his fellow Indians.*

Boom, that's the hook. Controversh. If you haven't got their attention now, you might as well pack up and go home. Round two! A new opponent enters. In the red corner we have: B. R. Ambedkar. Say B. R. Ambedkar. And yeah, hundred per cent I know I'm schooling Mrs L because how would she have heard of him? I only found out about him, like, two months ago. Ambedkar, this Dalit, this untouchable, who beat all the odds, educated himself, rose to the highest ranks of the independence movement and drafted India's first ever constitution versus The Mahatma himself. Ambedkar swings first – has the balls to say Gandhi doesn't speak for the Dalits, because he isn't one. Has the bare cheek to write a whole speech about how you can't reform the caste system, it has inequality baked into the very core. That shit has to be blown up and you have to start again.

High-caste Hindus wouldn't eat with Dalits. Wouldn't let them live in their neighbourhoods, use the same water fountains, pray in the same temples… So how come Gandhi's so against Dalits having separate elections in the new India, free from high-caste intimidation? Wham! Democracy is supposed to serve the people, not the other way round, right? *Ambedkar said 'I want political power for my community. That is indispensible for our survival.'* Mrs L said that one spoke to her from history.

But Gandhi's squaring up, boxing clever. He *hates* Ambedkar's speech. Thinks high-caste Hindus just need a bit of hand-holding to get them to see Dalits as human beings. Thinks if the issue's forced there'll be violence, bloodshed. Ambedkar counters: Dalits' rights can't wait. But Gandhi lands his killer blow and starts fasting. And like I said, that man can *fast*. Ambedkar looks around, sees a force-ten tornado coming right at him. What if Gandhi goes all out? What if he *dies*? Ambedkar's entire community would be blamed. And you *know* whose blood would be shed then, right?

So Ambedkar concedes to Gandhi. His speech, 'The Annihilation of Caste', is never heard. You can read it online though, and he says in the intro he's not a *'persona grata'*. Someone 'acceptable'. I looked it up. *So, in conclusion, the pen can be mightier than the sword, but it isn't always clear if the right person wins, or even gets to speak in the first place. (To* BETTINA.) I got eighty-five per cent.

BETTINA. Nice.

ASHA. Correct and appropriate use of archival materials – tick. Good understanding of the interpretations put forward in the extract – tick. Well-supported and convincing evaluation of the arguments – tick, tick, tick. Mrs L said, between me and her, it was the best mock exam paper she'd seen in all her years. Straight up, thought she was going to cry.

BETTINA. Lolz. Knocked it out Sunday evening between *Assassin's Creed* sessions, didn't you?

ASHA. Haha. Yeah… *(Direct address.) No.* Spent two weeks doing research and pulled three all-nighters writing three, no… *four* drafts… I sort of get lost in stuff, if it's something I haven't heard about before? Takes me a bit of time to work out what I think about it and it helps if I can get it all down on paper.

BETTINA. You told Mum yet?

ASHA. She won't give a shit. *(Direct address.)* Like, Mrs L said she only started to really enjoy history after she discovered Emmeline Pankhurst, which is cool, but then she said I should draw on my personal experience more often too, and that was just weird.

BETTINA. Mum'll be made up. This one's close to her heart, isn't it? Gandhi and that.

ASHA. She grew up in Evington.

BETTINA. I mean, it's about our… you know, our roots, and stuff?

ASHA (*direct address*). Mum read the final draft before I handed it in. She found a printout on the dining table when she was clearing up before dinner. Went batshit. *Forbid* me from submitting it. Can you believe that? Kept saying who was I to slag off Gandhiji? How I'd got soft in the head. Been spending too much time on TikTok. Is this what influencers were telling me? Poisoning my mind against actual independence heroes. Said I should be ashamed. Said *she* was ashamed. Real talk, I thought she was going to have a stroke or something. Told me I had to rewrite it. Like, this is literally the day before the deadline. How the hell was I supposed to do that?

BETTINA. She's on nights this week, you know? If we don't head back now we won't catch her before work.

ASHA. You'd better go, then.

BETTINA. We could walk?

ASHA. Why're you so interested in how I get home?

BETTINA. Want to show you something.

ASHA. What?

  BETTINA *pulls her phone out of her bag. She scrolls for a moment, looking for a photo.*

  (*Direct address.*) And thing is, when she gets like that my words freeze up, you know?… Ambedkar just wanted equality for his people, but it didn't sound the same out loud as it does on paper, and she did that thing where she acted as if I'd said something bare aggro even though I wasn't trying to argue with her, I was just trying to explain…

BETTINA (*holding out her phone*). This.

ASHA. What…? What am I looking at, exactly?

BETTINA. It's so cute. Look at its little nose.

ASHA. What is it?

BETTINA. It's in the window of the pet shop on the high street.

ASHA. Right...

BETTINA. He only wants thirty-four ninety-nine for the cage and the sawdust and the food.

ASHA. Oh my days...

BETTINA. Mrs Gopal gives you five pounds an hour now.

ASHA. She doesn't just give it me, I have to work for it, don't I?

BETTINA. Whenever I come in you've got your nose in a book.

ASHA. She doesn't mind if it's quiet.

BETTINA. Just five pounds. Please? I'm only five pounds short.

ASHA. You're carrying *thirty* quid around on you?

BETTINA. Been saving up. I'm *so* close.

ASHA. Answer's no.

BETTINA. I'll keep it on my side of the room. They're really clean.

ASHA. They're vermin.

BETTINA. That's not true.

ASHA. Mum will not let you have a hamster.

BETTINA. She will if you explain it to her.

ASHA. Explain what?

BETTINA. She's always stressed at the moment.

ASHA. She doesn't need a hamster, she needs a raise.

BETTINA. Statistics show having a pet reduces your risk of allergies and promotes personal well-being.

ASHA. I think that only works if you *like* animals.

BETTINA. She likes animals.

ASHA. No she doesn't.

BETTINA. She always stops to pet cats.

ASHA. Cats eat hamsters.

BETTINA. I'll clean it out, twice a week. I'll take really good care of it. I promise. They're super quiet. And they're *really* affectionate.

BETTINA *holds her phone out again.*

ASHA. That's not a hamster. It's too big to be a hamster. It's like… I dunno… That's a guinea pig or something.

BETTINA. Please, Asha? Just come and have a look at it with me?

ASHA. No.

BETTINA. It's on the way home.

ASHA. I'm not going home yet.

BETTINA. Why?

ASHA. *Because.*

BETTINA. How long you going to stay here for?

ASHA (*direct address*). Last thing Mum said to me was how Mrs L would be angry too if I did the same thing to any of her heroes. Like, the suffragettes, or something.

BETTINA. Just five pounds?

ASHA. *No.* (*Direct address.*) And I was like, 'Maybe that's the problem, Mum, you're making out Gandhi's some sort of saint and I'm going to be struck by lightning or something for daring to question him.' And that was the *wrong* thing to say because she clammed up and it's been like that ever since.

BETTINA. It's getting dark.

ASHA. What time is it?

BETTINA (*checks her watch*). Five-thirty.

ASHA *gathers together her things and puts on her jacket.*

You'll come then? To the pet shop?

ASHA. No. I'm going through the park.

BETTINA. You're going the long way?

ASHA. Yeah.

BETTINA. Why?

ASHA. Mind your own business for once, yeah?

BETTINA. Wow. Excuse me for breathing.

Scene Two

Two weeks later, ASHA *is cleaning graffiti off the gates at the front of the school, headphones on.* BETTINA *enters.*

BETTINA. What happened?

ASHA. What?

ASHA *has to take her headphones off to hear her.*

BETTINA. You in detention?

ASHA. What's it look like?

BETTINA. You're not allowed headphones in detention.

ASHA. You going to tell on me?

BETTINA. No. (*Of the cleaner.*) It'll come off easier if you use that one.

ASHA. What?

BETTINA. You want the kind that smells like oranges? And… a brush with hard bristles. Like this one.

ASHA. Did I ask for your advice?

BETTINA. You need an oil-based cleaner for an oil-based paint.

ASHA. Did I ask for your *help*?

BETTINA. Otherwise you're creating an emulsion.

ASHA. What do you know about emulsions?

BETTINA. We did them in Chemistry.

ASHA. It's coming off.

BETTINA. *Bare* slow, though. Bus'll be here in fifteen minutes.

ASHA. Don't miss it.

   BETTINA *sits down, takes out a bag of crisps from her bag. Offers* ASHA *one.*

   No thanks.

BETTINA. Why'd you paint it?

ASHA. I didn't.

BETTINA.…Then why're you cleaning it?

ASHA. Because I'm a good Samaritan.

BETTINA. What?

ASHA. Because I'm a community champion.

BETTINA. How come you're in detention?

ASHA. Because Mrs L's a bitch.

BETTINA. She's always seemed alright to me.

ASHA. Used to think so too.

BETTINA. She's friendly in the playground.

ASHA. Not the same as being in her class. She's different with the little kids.

BETTINA. I'm not a little kid.

ASHA. Year 10 is little.

BETTINA. So you're not in detention for tagging the gates?

ASHA. As if.

BETTINA. What did you do, then?

ASHA. You're going to miss your bus.

BETTINA. I'll go if you tell me what you did.

ASHA. Didn't do anything.

BETTINA. So why're you in detention?

ASHA. It was stupid. I kicked off with Mel Summers in the common room.

BETTINA. Serious?

ASHA. Yes.

BETTINA. Why?

ASHA. Nothing… Over a bag of Quavers.

BETTINA. A bag of Quavers?

ASHA. So go wait at the bus stop now, yeah?

BETTINA. I'll get the next one. You'll be done by then.

ASHA. I'm not getting the bus with you.

BETTINA. Why not?

ASHA. Going round Rommi's on the way home.

BETTINA. I'll wait for you.

ASHA. You're always *around*. Every step I take, you're right there, behind me.

BETTINA. Yeah, I've *literally* got your back.

ASHA. I don't need it, thanks.

> ASHA *tries to push her towards the bus stop.* BETTINA *doesn't budge, showing impressive passive resistance. Hurt beat.* BETTINA *straightens her jacket, etc.*

> Why don't you go home and watch telly or something?

BETTINA. Sana and Adeel and that lot get that bus.

ASHA. So…?

BETTINA.… You'll be pissed at me.

ASHA. What have they been doing?

BETTINA. They've been making me pay an extra fare. To go upstairs.

ASHA. An upstairs fare?

BETTINA. Mm-hmm.

ASHA. So you've been telling them to fuck off, right?

BETTINA. No.

ASHA. Why not?

BETTINA. It's easy for you to say.

ASHA. It's easy for anyone to say. Fuck and off. There. Try it.

BETTINA. I started sitting downstairs. Near the front, where the driver is. And that worked for a bit. But now they're charging me a door fare.

ASHA. A door fare?

BETTINA. Yeah.

ASHA. As in, when you want to get off?

BETTINA. Yeah.

ASHA. And this time you definitely told them to fuck off, right?

BETTINA. If I tell them to fuck off I'll get slaps.

ASHA. Adeel? Adeel Adeel?

BETTINA. ... Yes.

ASHA. Who used to live on Glenmore?

BETTINA. Yes.

ASHA. There's nothing to him. He's a beanpole. You're scared of *him*?

BETTINA. He's bulked out, yeah? He's been going to the green gym.

ASHA. He heads straight to Quran school in the afternoon, doesn't he?

BETTINA. Not any more.

ASHA. You tried talking to him?

BETTINA. *No*. What's the point?

ASHA. You don't know if you don't try?

BETTINA. I'm not like you.

ASHA. What's that supposed to mean?

BETTINA. I don't always know the right thing to say. Anyway Adeel's not the worst. He just joins in with the others because he's such a loser.

Beat.

Been using my birthday money but it's run out now.

ASHA. Thirty quid? They've taken *thirty quid* off you…?

BETTINA. Don't tell Mum.

ASHA. She's going to lose it. How much does she pay for your bus pass?

BETTINA. I know.

ASHA. And now she's paying *double*.

BETTINA. I *know*.

ASHA. Because of Sana, Lee and skinny-ass Adeel…?

BETTINA. He's not skinny any more. And they wouldn't dare if they thought you were going to back me up. Especially after you kicked Mel Summers' butt in the common room.

ASHA. It wasn't like that.

BETTINA. It got physical though…?

ASHA. Well, yeah… Sort of…

BETTINA. Hundred per cent. Bet you landed on her like a drone strike. Eyes blazing. Slapped her until her head was spinning.

ASHA. No.

BETTINA. Bet you were like *fire*. Righteous *fire*.

ASHA. I didn't go into the common room looking for Mel, or looking for trouble, or looking for *anyone*.

BETTINA. Oh come on, Asha. As if you'd lose it over a bag of Quavers?

BETTINA *offers up her crisps again, but* ASHA *doesn't notice.*

ASHA (*direct address*). Mum blanked me all through breakfast and I was tired of it. Then just before I left I told her we had a new assignment and she said 'What're you going to write to suck up to Mrs L this time?' She can be so harsh, man. So I was thinking what *should* I write? How can I 'draw on my personal experience', like Mrs L said? Except not piss off Mum this time? And what did she mean 'personal'? Like, Gandhiji? Or Ambedkar? I mean, they're a couple of dudes. *Old* dudes. *Dead* dudes. And why wouldn't Emmeline Pankhurst be my experience? She's dead too. Was Mum right? Like, Mrs L has dibs on Pankhurst and co. so I should leave well alone…? I'd ask Mum but she's not talking to me, is she?

BETTINA.…*You* could tell them to fuck off?

ASHA. What?

BETTINA. Adeel and Sana and that lot?

ASHA. You need me to do that for you?

BETTINA. And maybe you could, like, push them around a bit?

ASHA. I'm not pushing Adeel around. Known him since he was in nappies.

BETTINA. Sana then.

ASHA. You want me to get on the bus and beat up Sana? In front of everyone?

BETTINA. It doesn't have to be on the bus. It could be out here. Or… or… in the common room again? That would be good. Yeah, that would really send a *message*.

ASHA. And then what?

BETTINA.…They leave me alone and I start saving up again.

ASHA. And then what for *me*?

Beat. BETTINA *looks at all the cleaning products, and the graffiti.*

BETTINA. Just get on the bus with me, then. They only have to *think* we're tight. That you like me.

ASHA. I do like you.

BETTINA. So why won't you do it, then?

ASHA. You know this is the first time I've ever been in detention? And, like, I've been close time and time again. Lost count of how many yellow cards I've been on. But I always pull it right from the brink.

BETTINA. Course you do. Make it look easy.

ASHA. Yeah, but it's not, is it? And now I've got a suspension on my school record, three months before I'm going to send out my UCAS. And I'm not risking getting another one just so you can buy a guinea pig.

BETTINA. It's a hamster.

ASHA. It's too *big* to be a hamster.

BETTINA. Shit, you know they're choosing people for the leavers' assembly now?

ASHA. ...Are they?

BETTINA. Yeah. Three spots. Was in this week's newsletter.

ASHA. I don't read the newsletter.

BETTINA. Apparently they've got this new PA system in De Montfort Hall and the orchestra are going to sound amazing.

ASHA. Right.

BETTINA (*of the graffiti, etc*). They'll still give you a spot, yeah?

ASHA. ...Don't have a god-given right, do I?

BETTINA. You're the smartest kid in school.

ASHA. No I'm not.

BETTINA. Who's smarter?

ASHA (*direct address*). So I started thinking to myself, would I get an eighty-five per cent doing the same to Emmeline and her crew? Would Mrs L still appreciate my critical analysis? Like, yeah, I know it sounds kind of disloyal, but I want Mum to be wrong so bad. And I don't know that much about the suffragettes. Only that woman who jumped in front of the King's horse. And I've found out she had a return ticket home and didn't mean to get trampled, so now I'm like, shit, what else don't I know? So I've been reading up about the suffragettes, and the First World Wwar, and all this stuff about one of Emmeline's daughters, Sylvia, is coming up. She said stuff like… 'every war of modern times has been fought with the purely materialistic object of forwarding the schemes and protecting the interests of powerful and wealthy financiers'. Bankers, she means bankers. I looked it up. *Bare* reminds me of Ambedkar. I'm thinking Sylvia would definitely be in his corner, right? But Emmeline and Christabel, Sylvia's sister, they drop the campaign for women's suffrage when the war breaks out. Go all-out for army recruitment instead. Hundred per cent they're in Gandhi's corner, yeah? This fight was so real the suffragettes in Britain split. K'Od. Straight up. Sylvia saw women's suffrage as just the start – she wanted to 'create a society where there are no rich or poor, no people without work or beauty in their lives, where money itself will disappear, where we shall all be brothers and sisters, where everyone will have enough'. That didn't include getting your head blown off on some battlefield, yeah? But other people, even her mum and her sister, looked at what shc was saying, and thought it was unrealistic.

BETTINA. This is partly your fault anyway.

ASHA.…What?

BETTINA. In a… way.

ASHA. How'd you work that one out?

BETTINA. If you'd just lent me the five pounds last week I'd be chilling at home with my hamster right now.

ASHA. It is *not* my fault. (*Direct address*.) And I'm in the queue in the common room, just trying to buy some Quavers.

And I'm thinking how Emmeline and Christabel let Sylvia down. And you know, maybe they sort of let us all down... But what if Mum's right, about Mrs L only wanting me to talk about brown dudes? Nah... That's not it, either. About Mrs L only being comfortable with me *criticising* brown dudes? I need two As and a B for Goldsmiths. Do I really want to risk that? And then, all of a sudden, I get a fist in my back – sharp, right in my spine, so it bare hurts. And I realise the queue's moved on in front of me. And Mel Summers is right behind me and she whispers, so only I can hear her, 'Get a move on, Paki.' And I don't even stop to think, I turn around and push her, both hands on her chest, bam!

BETTINA. Just lend me a couple of quid, then? So I've got a bit extra?

ASHA. So you can hand it over to Sana and Adeel?

BETTINA. See it as... an investment in my well-being.

ASHA. Protection money?

BETTINA. Don't you want to protect me?

ASHA. You need to fight your own battles, Bettina.

BETTINA. I'll tell Mum what happened in the common room.

ASHA. You don't know jack shit.

BETTINA. What did she do? Did she call you a bitch or something?

ASHA.... Yeah.

BETTINA. Serves her right then, doesn't it?

ASHA. Mrs L was all 'I'm really disappointed in you, Asha', and 'I'm not sure you've considered how actions like this could impact upon your future.'

BETTINA. She knows there must have been a reason, yeah? Like, you're not the kind of person who's going to lash out like some sort of animal?

ASHA (*direct address*). And I wasn't sure what she meant at first. Like, what's she saying? I'm not going Goldsmiths because I pushed Mel Summers over in the common room?

Mel's making out she's like, sustained serious injuries or
something. And Mrs L's taken the bait. Says I need to learn
to control my temper. Says I should know better than to
resort to violence. I tell her there're some things that
shouldn't be tolerated. The P-word being one of those things.
But Mel denies it and it's my word against hers and Mrs L
gets bare angry and puts us both on detention. And when
I say that's not fair, she says Mel's being punished too.
Except how is it teaching Mel a lesson if I'm being made to
do exactly the same thing?

BETTINA. I won't say anything to Mum. If she asks I'll tell her
you were studying late. At the library. Or round Rommi's.

ASHA. Tell her what you want. She'll find out anyway. And
I'm not getting the bus with you. Have to clean all this.

BETTINA (*picking up a sponge*). I can help you.

ASHA. I don't want you to.

Beat.

BETTINA. I got your back, Asha. Even if you don't have mine.

BETTINA *starts to clean the other end of the gates, as far
away from* ASHA *as possible.*

ASHA *puts her headphones in and continues scrubbing the
gates.*

Scene Three

Three days later. BETTINA *sits at the bus stop outside the school gates, which already have fresh graffiti on them.* ASHA *joins her, headphones in.*

ASHA (*taking one headphone out so she can listen to BETTINA too*). You heading home?

BETTINA. Yeah… Waiting for the next bus.

ASHA. I'll wait with you.

BETTINA. You don't have to. Sana and Adeel and that lot got on the last one.

ASHA. I'm coming anyway.

BETTINA.…Alright.

> BETTINA *opens a bag of crisps.* ASHA *gets a book out of her bag and starts to read.*

What're you reading?

> ASHA *shows* BETTINA *the cover.*

Any good?

ASHA. I've got to gen up on the Magna Carta for my coursework. So boring, man.

BETTINA. Why're you doing it, then?

ASHA. Need a dead-cert eighty-five per cent to keep my average up. Talked it through with Mum.

BETTINA. Mum said you should do the Magna Carta?

ASHA. No… But she says it's a safe bet. Go heavy on the liberty, rights and justice stuff. Make all the right noises but avoid the nitty-gritty.

BETTINA. Like throwing shade on Gandhi?

ASHA. I didn't throw shade on Gandhi. She says I just need to turn in a solid, well-researched essay with no conjecture or hot takes. Stay on track ahead of my UCAS. Put all the aggro in the common room behind me. She said when she was my age they did King John at school and she did this big project

on him signing the Magna Carta and she'd help me with
mine if I wanted to do that too. Couldn't exactly turn around
and say no, could I?

BETTINA. She's well excited about the leavers' assembly.

ASHA. I know. Wants to help me find a poem to submit.

BETTINA. Told me she's going to get a new dress.

ASHA. She shouldn't.

BETTINA. No stopping her.

ASHA. They haven't even said who'll be speaking yet.

BETTINA. Least she's talking to you again.

ASHA. … Yeah.

BETTINA. Thank god.

ASHA. All I've got to do is exactly what she says.

BETTINA. Tell me about it.

ASHA. What're you chatting about? You always get a free ride.

BETTINA. Because she barely notices me.

ASHA. That is not true.

BETTINA. I don't care anyway. Six months' time, me and
Cardi'll have a room to ourselves.

ASHA. Cardi?

BETTINA. Yeah. My hamster.

ASHA. Why Cardi?

BETTINA. She's got a cute little nose.

ASHA (*direct address*). I've found all this stuff online. About
this magazine Christabel ran, and how she started slagging
Sylvia off after the war broke out. Saying shit like 'I consider
the pacifists a disease – a very deadly disease.' *Sylvia* was a
pacifist. That's her own sister she was talking about.

BETTINA. What're you listening to?

ASHA. Kendrick Lamar. (*Direct address*.) And Ambedkar said himself he was the 'most hated man in Hindu India'. So maybe Mum's right and I should keep my head down for a bit.

BETTINA. The new one? Let me hear?

ASHA. No...

BETTINA *pulls out* ASHA's *headphones. The audiobook* ASHA's *been listening to blares out from her phone.*

NARRATOR (*voice-over*). 'They aimed to make 198 Bow Road a political home of hope for the women and children of the district. Sylvia describes how they scrubbed and polished the interior until it was spotless.'

BETTINA. That is not Kendrick Lamar.

ASHA. No, alright...

ASHA *goes to turn it off but* BETTINA *stops her.*

BETTINA. Wait.

NARRATOR (*voice-over*). 'She climbed a wooden tower scaffold and painted the legend "VOTES FOR WOMEN" on the shopfront in elegantly gilded characters. As she worked, an intrigued throng gathered around her. The real, expensive gold leaf she had used gleamed in striking contrast to the soot, dirt and dilapidation around the old bakery, reflecting the brightness and energy of the crowd. The lustrous classic Roman lettering, freshly painted shopfront and sparkling windows sent a clear, inviting message – nothing here is too good for the women workers.'

BETTINA. What's this?

ASHA. Audiobook I found about Sylvia Pankhurst.

BETTINA. Who?

ASHA. Would've written about her. If I wasn't doing this Magna Carta thing.

BETTINA. Why're you listening to it, then?

ASHA. Trying to have a quiet moment while I wait for the bus, aren't I?

BETTINA (*of Magna Carta book*). Shouldn't you be concentrating on that?

ASHA. I am.

BETTINA. Multitasking is a myth, you know? The human brain is only capable of focusing on one thing at a time. Saw it on this documentary.

ASHA. You spend too much time on YouTube.

BETTINA. Where did she work then?

ASHA. What?

BETTINA. 'Nothing's too good for women workers.'

ASHA. They don't mean her exactly... Look, I found photos...

She shows BETTINA *a photo on her phone.*

BETTINA. That's her painting the sign?

ASHA. Yeah. She's setting up the place *for* women workers.

BETTINA. To do what?

ASHA. You know. Fight for their rights.

BETTINA. To do what?

ASHA.... Everything. They didn't even have the vote back then.

BETTINA. What's that got to do with her cleaning windows?

ASHA. She wanted them to know she saw them as equal... No, I mean, she wanted them to see *themselves* as equal.

BETTINA. To who?

ASHA. Everyone. And... she wanted the world to be like that. And she believed you could only make it happen if you started doing it yourself. And look, here's one of her giving a speech afterwards.

ASHA *shows her another photo on her phone.*

Feels like she could be giving it right here, right now, doesn't it?

BETTINA. She's in black and white.

ASHA. Apart from that.

BETTINA. Why aren't you writing about her?

ASHA. ...I can't.

BETTINA. Because of Mum?

ASHA. It's more complicated than that.

BETTINA. Mr Fitzpatrick leant me this book by Malala Yousafzai.

ASHA. Why?

BETTINA. I kicked off in Geography about our textbooks.

ASHA. You kicked off?

BETTINA. Yeah.

ASHA. What did you say?

BETTINA. We were learning about the difference between asylum seekers, refugees, and migrants, and I said the government invented those words and seeing as they still aren't doing anything about climate change, we shouldn't listen to them on this one either.

ASHA. You said that to Fitzpatrick?

BETTINA. Yeah.

ASHA. Why?

BETTINA. Cos then Sana and Adeel and that lot would hear about it and maybe they'd think I'm a badass and stop picking on me. But Fitzpatrick just got really excited and started this long discussion about how borders are man-made and how we change them all the time, even recently, like in Mexico and Texas. And he kept me behind after class to recommend some websites and loan me Malala.

ASHA. You shouldn't go looking for trouble. You're in enough of it already.

BETTINA. That's what I keep saying. Except you won't help, will you, so what else am I supposed to do?

ASHA. ...Just don't understand why you're putting yourself through all this aggro for a *guinea pig*.

BETTINA. It's not a guinea pig.

ASHA. It is not a hamster either, Bettina. It's too big to be a hamster.

BETTINA. I know it's a hamster, because I had a dream about it. I had a dream it was running and running, you know, on the little wheel they have? And it was scared, because it knew something was following it. Not actually following it, in the pet shop. But somewhere, out there, something was after it, and even though it didn't make any sense, it had to run, it just had to. Because that was the only way to get rid of the panic it could feel setting in. And when I woke up my heart was *pounding* and I was out of breath.

ASHA. You think you're a hamster?

BETTINA. No... I just mean... It's scared, and I want to bring it home and look after it. Their hearts beat fast because they're so little, you know that? The smaller you are, the quicker your heart beats. But it doesn't matter what size your heart is, we all only get an average of about two billion beats over our lifetime. It's just a pump at the end of the day, right? And all these pumps, they give up after two billion beats. That's why littler animals don't live as long. Their hearts have been beating faster the whole time, so two billion beats comes a lot quicker for them.

ASHA. You're not that short.

BETTINA. Haha.

ASHA. Like, you're short, but it's not going to make that big a difference. Not so you'll notice. When your time comes.

BETTINA. When I get on the bus, my heart beats so fast I swear everyone can hear it. Even the driver, behind the plastic screen. That's how loud it is. And then I get so embarrassed it beats harder. And faster. And that happens every day.

ASHA. It just feels like that.

BETTINA. What if it's not just my birthday money they're taking? What if they're like... taking away my *life*.

ASHA. You don't have to be so dramatic all the time.

BETTINA. What if every time they pick on me it's shaving, I dunno, three days off the end for me? Like, three thousand beats or something.

ASHA. It's not that serious.

BETTINA. What, not like your boring essay about the Magna Carta?

ASHA. What's that supposed to mean?

BETTINA. Let me see those photos again.

BETTINA *grabs* ASHA*'s phone.*

ASHA. Bettina.

BETTINA. You want to be her in the second photo but you don't want to be her in the first one. Don't want to roll your sleeves up and actually get your hands dirty. You're all talk, Asha.

ASHA. What are you on…?

BETTINA. What's the point of all these dry quotes about justice and liberty if you won't even help your own kid sister when she's getting taxed on the bus? Got to start somewhere? Try starting *here*, yeah?

ASHA. Alright, alright. Chill.

BETTINA. You're being *too* chill, Asha. That's my point.

ASHA. Okay. Look, far as I can see, you've got three options. One, do what they want, which you're already doing.

BETTINA. Sort of, yeah.

ASHA. Which you're *actually* doing, you're doing exactly what they want without so much as a peep. It's pathetic.

BETTINA. Alright. You don't have to be mean about it.

ASHA. Two, fight back.

BETTINA. That's what you'd do.

ASHA. I'd do *something*.

BETTINA. Except they wouldn't pick on you in the first place.

ASHA. They might have done… When I was in Year 10.

BETTINA. So how did you stop being that kid?

ASHA. What kid?

BETTINA. A kid like me.

ASHA. ... You don't want to stop being *you*.

BETTINA. It's easy for you to say, you're not getting picked on every day.

ASHA. Why don't you do this to Sana and Adeel? Argue with them until they lose the will to live?

BETTINA. If I annoy them I'll get slaps.

ASHA. So that leaves option three. Act like you're doing what they want, but really do what *you* want. Box clever. Play it *smart*.

BETTINA. Is that what you're doing, then?

ASHA. What?

BETTINA. Writing about the Magna Carta?

ASHA. It's not the same.

BETTINA. So you're just doing what they want?

ASHA. Whatever. (*Direct address.*) I mean, Mum's talking to me again, yeah? *Really* talking to me. Telling me stuff I've never known before. So what am I supposed to do? She told me about this friend she had, growing up. Her best friend. Mariam. How they totally bonded, right from reception, did everything together. They had this pact to go to the same uni, get a flatshare, the works. But then they grew apart in their last year in sixth form because Mariam started to have weirder and weirder views. Started playing up in class. Finding trouble where there wasn't any. Fell out with all the teachers, even Mrs Osbourne who did English Literature and Mum loved her. She was reading all these books and pamphlets. Stuff she would've got into bare trouble for if anyone else knew. Mum reckons if it happened now people would say she was being 'radicalised'. Mum tried talking to her and Mariam tried to push her away. But Mum says you don't leave it like that, not if you love someone. She kept

talking to her, giving her other stuff to read, and eventually
Mariam came around. Sorted herself out. It was just a phase,
but if it wasn't for Mum this phase could've really fucked
things up for her. I knew why Mum was telling me this.
I was Mariam. I got it. I'm not stupid. She's like 'Play the
game, Asha. You're smart enough to understand that.' But
even though she's telling me all this stuff, confiding in me, it
just feels like I'm being told to shut up. (*To* BETTINA.) So
you get on the bus, yeah?

ASHA *pretends she's* BETTINA.

Sana and Adeel see you getting on. (*She motions that*
BETTINA*'s now Sana and Adeel.*)

BETTINA (*changing her stance*). They sit at the back. Real
spread out, taking up four, six seats. They see *everything*.

ASHA. What do they say when they see *you*?

BETTINA. They start giggling first. Whispering about me.
I can't hear what they're saying.

ASHA. Right.

BETTINA. Then they're like… (*Pretends to be Sana and Adeel,
mock-friendly.*) 'Bettina! Hey Bettina! We saved a seat for
you. Come on. Been waiting for you.'

ASHA. And what do you do?

BETTINA. Give them the finger…?

ASHA. Really?

BETTINA. Yeah.

ASHA. Thought you were too scared to stand up to them?

BETTINA. It's only for show, though.

ASHA *pretends to be* BETTINA, *trying to look surly,
flipping the bird.*

I sit as far away from them as possible, but it doesn't matter
where I go, they'll come over and sit right behind me. And
they'll be like 'Sorry, Bettina, think you've forgotten
something?' And I know what they mean so I try to ignore
them, but one of them, usually Sana, will start jabbing me in

the ribs. Hard, so it hurts. But bare subtle, so no one notices. You know?

ASHA. ...Like even she knows what she's doing is shameful, so she does it on the quiet. Coward move.

BETTINA. For real.

ASHA. So what do you do?

BETTINA. I try to push her off me. And she's like 'What're you being so aggressive for? Just trying to be friendly.' And then I'll try to get up but one of them'll block me. And they know when my stop's coming and I know they won't let me get off unless I give them some cash.

ASHA. You don't say anything?

BETTINA. Once I shouted at them to fuck off and leave me alone, but a lady told me to stop swearing in front of her kid, and Sana and Adeel and that lot acted all shocked and innocent. Made out I was the bad guy.

ASHA. Right, so you need to show you're scared.

BETTINA. So they can laugh at me even more?

ASHA. Not Sana and Adeel and that lot. You need everyone *else* on the bus to know you're scared. Right now they're turning up the volume on their earphones. Pretending to read their book. Last thing they want to do is get involved. You need to show how scared you are. Like anyone would be. Just like you've been telling me. That your heart's beating too fast. That you want to cry. You just want them to leave you alone. Dial it up.

BETTINA. So, like, play the victim?

ASHA. *Yes*. You can borrow one of my shirts and my spare blazer tomorrow.

BETTINA. Why?

ASHA. So you'll look all little and cute and harmless in your oversized uniform. You need to drill it in that you're pathetic and if no one does anything, bad shit's going to go down and they're going to regret it.

BETTINA. Like what?

ASHA. I dunno… Leave it to their imaginations.

BETTINA. You think that'll work?

ASHA.… Yeah.

BETTINA. You sure?

ASHA. Yeah. And if it gets really hairy, just start crying and press the emergency stop.

BETTINA. Okay.

BETTINA *exits.* ASHA *plays the audiobook again.*

NARRATOR (*voice-over*). 'In the great chaos and tortuous convolutions of this unbodied thing we call Capitalism, wherein too often we are as corks, tossed on the ocean, all this was vague, amorphous. How could one make it plain to those whose untutored minds craved only for curt, neat slogans?'

ASHA (*direct address*). I feel that, yeah? Deep. Cowards, they whisper. Right?

ASHA *looks at her book on Magna Carta. She closes it decisively, and stashes it away in her rucksack. She plays the audiobook again.*

NARRATOR (*voice-over*). 'Aware that her pacifism for the moment put her in a minority position, Sylvia decided to bide her time until public anti-war sentiment developed. It was yet early days. She knew she wouldn't have to wait long before the realities hit.'

Scene Four

Next afternoon. BETTINA *finds* ASHA *outside the school gates. She's wearing* ASHA*'s school blouse and blazer, two sizes too big for her.*

BETTINA. I'm getting the bus. By myself. I'm getting the bus by myself. (*She pulls a five-pound note from her purse.*) I can get on the bus waving this around. I can… (*She makes a neat triangle out of it and tucks it into the top pocket of her blazer.*) get on the bus like this. I can get on like –

BETTINA *starts to jubilantly rap/sing Cardi B's 'Money'.* ASHA *joins in – they know all the words. They dance, have a pose-off, and* ASHA *makes it rain with her revision cards. They take the opportunity to revel in this incredible victory.*

ASHA. It go okay, then?

BETTINA. Yeah.

ASHA. What happened?

BETTINA. I got on and they were like – (*Pretending to be Sana and Adeel.*) 'Here she is! Bettina, our queen! Yass! Saved a seat for you. Come over, babes.' And usually I'd try and front it out but this time I just acted how I felt. I was like 'Please don't hurt me. You can have my money if you want, but please stop hurting me. I can't take it any more.'

ASHA. You said that?

BETTINA. That was the gist of it. And first of all they started laughing, so I ramped it up. Started telling this lady next to me what they've been doing. (*Hamming it up.*) 'I was going to get a hamster but they've taken all my birthday money, and who knows what they've spent it on? And if my mum finds out she's going to kill me. I don't know what to do.'

BETTINA *pauses to make puppy-dog eyes at* ASHA, *maybe even pretends to cry.*

ASHA. Heartbreaking shit.

BETTINA. And this lady makes room on the seat next to her and has a go at Sana and Adeel, telling them they should be ashamed of themselves, and she'll call the police if they hassle me again, and how I'd be within my rights to call the police *now* if I wanted to, and maybe then they'd learn a lesson, because they obviously weren't learning anything at school. And the whole bus was *bare* quiet, and this lady gave me a Polo, and when we got to my stop the bus driver made a big show of stopping for ages, and getting out of his seat to wave me off and making sure Sana and Adeel didn't follow me.

ASHA. And the Oscar goes to…

BETTINA. It just all came out, yeah? Everything they've pulled for the past… what? *Two* months? Torturing me. Making life a living hell. So now I can start saving again and in a month I'll be able to bring Cardi home.

ASHA. Sweet.

BETTINA. I know, right?

ASHA. I'm really pleased for you.

BETTINA. I've got you to thank for this, you know?

ASHA. I don't think so.

BETTINA. No way I'd have been brave enough to do that if you hadn't prepped me. You and Susan.

ASHA. Sylvia.

BETTINA. You get your essay back from Mrs L?

ASHA. Yep.

BETTINA. Smash that eighty-five per cent again?

ASHA. Nope.

BETTINA. Thought the Magna Carta was safe territory?

ASHA. Didn't do it about the Magna Carta.

BETTINA. Ohhhh… Why not?

ASHA.…Didn't feel like it.

BETTINA. What did you get?

> ASHA *gets the essay out of her bag and slides it over to* BETTINA.

> Sixty-five per cent?

ASHA. First time I've ever got below a B-plus. And Mrs L put all these picky notes in red, about where my quotes came from, and about my grammar, and even my spelling when it was obviously just a typo or two. So I called her out on it after class.

BETTINA. Shiiiit. Really?

ASHA. Waited until it was just me and her.

BETTINA. What did you say?

ASHA. I said she was marking with unconscious bias and it wasn't on.

BETTINA. Fuuuuuuck.

ASHA. And she said she was a fair marker, and I should think very carefully before making accusations like that because they are very serious. But that was the whole point. That's why I said it. Because it is very serious.

BETTINA. Hundred per cent.

ASHA. And she just said, and she wasn't really listening to me, not really, I could tell. She said I was drawing on conjecture and speculation, taking quotes out of context and misrepresenting historical figures who have no right of reply.

BETTINA. Right of reply?

ASHA. It's not my fault they're dead. She said this quote I used about 'pacifists' referred to a movement, not an individual, and if anything *I* was guilty of unconscious bias because I was falling into the trap of reducing the work of women political activists to soap opera.

BETTINA. She allowed to say that?

ASHA. And she said I'd strayed too far from the essay title and if I did that under exam conditions the external examiner would be a lot harsher than her so it was for my own good to learn the parameters. But she said I could see the evidence for her marking if I wanted to, and I said yeah okay.

BETTINA. Then what?

ASHA. I didn't really understand what I was looking at, but I couldn't say anything, could I? She said if I still felt strongly about it I was welcome to make a formal complaint.

BETTINA. You going to?

ASHA. What do you think?

BETTINA. You going to tell Mum?

ASHA. She's going to be well pissed. No way I'm speaking at the leavers' assembly now.

BETTINA. She's already bought a dress.

ASHA. What, like, something fancy? What'd she do that for?

BETTINA. Saw it in the sale and snapped it up. Said she's going to bag a seat in the front row, make sure she makes the photo in the *Leicester Mercury.*

ASHA. Why?

BETTINA. Because she's proud of you, you donkey.

ASHA. She won't be when she hears about this sixty-five per cent. Although she does love an 'I told you so'.

BETTINA. Magna Carta next, then?

ASHA. Don't know if I've got time to make my grades up now.

BETTINA. You always pull it out the bag, don't you?

ASHA. That's the thing. I don't know if I can just front it out any more…

BETTINA. How'd you mean?

ASHA goes to speak, but then realises she isn't ready to share everything with BETTINA.

ASHA (*direct address*). I worked out it was 2001 when Mum was in Year 13. And I started thinking, all this stuff with Mariam. Was that before 9/11, or after? Because I've read all this shit-scary stuff about Muslims getting attacked and losing their jobs and getting death threats and that, after the Twin Towers. But when I asked Mum she clammed up. Got bare shifty and tried to change the subject. I asked what happened to Mariam. And she said they'd reconnected a few years ago, on Facebook and Mariam was working at this big-shot uni now. And how that would never have happened if she hadn't grown up, stopped living in a fantasy land where she was such a rebel and everything was black and white. So I asked her which uni this was where Mariam worked? Maybe I should apply there? But she said she had to do something in the kitchen, and I know she was pretending, because when I went to look all she'd done was put the kettle on.

BETTINA. You okay, Asha?

ASHA. I've just been thinking… Maybe I don't need to go Goldsmiths if it means keeping quiet about things.

BETTINA. But you've wanted to go there for time.

ASHA. I know.

BETTINA. Quiet about what things?

ASHA. Like… Listen to this…

ASHA scrolls through her phone looking for a recording of Ambedkar.

BETTINA. Susan again?

ASHA. Sylvia. No. Ambedkar. He said one person one vote didn't mean shit if it wasn't one person one *value*.

BETTINA.…Right…?

ASHA. You get me?

BETTINA. Not really.

ASHA. Like, if people aren't treated equally we don't have a democracy. And that's on all of us. It's like a collective responsibility, yeah? He laid it all out in six points. Listen…

ASHA plays a recording of Ambedkar to BETTINA *on her phone.*

AMBEDKAR (*voice-over*). 'Public conscience means conscience which becomes agitated at every wrong, no matter who is the sufferer, and it means that everybody, whether he suffers that particular wrong or not, is prepared to join him in order to get him relieved.'

BETTINA. Right, yeah. I get it. I think.

ASHA. He said ideas are mortal, just like living things. They need watering or they'll wither and die... I don't want my ideas to wither and die.

BETTINA. Oh my god, you finally found someone on your level and he's ancient and dead. Congratulations, sis.

ASHA *puts her phone away.* BETTINA *goes to leave.*

ASHA. Where you going?

BETTINA. To get the bus. See you.

ASHA. Alright. Laters.

BETTINA *leaves.* ASHA *takes out her phone again. She quietly records herself.*

An idea needs propagation as much as a plant needs watering. Otherwise both will wither and die.

She plays the voicenote back to herself.

(*Voice-over.*) '...both will wither and die.'

Scene Five

The next day, after school. ASHA *finds* BETTINA *waiting at the bus stop.* BETTINA*'s reading a book and eating an apple.*

ASHA. Did they say they were going to hurt you, Bettina?

BETTINA. What? Who?

ASHA. Adeel and Sana and that lot? Did they threaten you?

BETTINA. Yeah, all the time. I told you.

ASHA. I mean like properly threaten you? Did they say they were going to cut you?

BETTINA. Cut me...?

ASHA. Did they pull a knife on you?

BETTINA. No.

ASHA. Did they tell you they had one?

BETTINA....Um...

ASHA. Or... show you one?

BETTINA. A knife?

ASHA. *Yes.*

BETTINA. Why?

ASHA. You see the Safer Schools Officer was in today?

BETTINA....Yeah... I mean... I thought she was here for a special assembly or something...

ASHA. She took Adeel out of class.

BETTINA. Because he was robbing my pocket money?

ASHA. I don't think so.

BETTINA. Why then?

ASHA. People are saying he was carrying a knife on the bus. Is that true? You've never said anything about a knife.

BETTINA. No...

ASHA. So it's not true?

BETTINA. I don't think so...

ASHA. You don't *think* so?

BETTINA. No...

ASHA. Bettina, if you thought they were ever going to pull a blade on you, you'd *remember.*

BETTINA. Yeah, yeah, you're right.

ASHA. So you haven't said that to anyone?

Beat.

BETTINA. Not to anyone at school...

BETTINA *comfort-eats.*

ASHA. Where then? On the bus?

BETTINA. Yeah… Maybe.

ASHA. Who did you say it to? The lady with the Polos, or the
bus driver?

BETTINA. The driver… No… The lady. It was the lady.

ASHA. What did you say?

BETTINA. I don't know.

ASHA. Imagine I'm her.

BETTINA. What…?

ASHA. Might help you remember.

BETTINA. She asked me… She asked me how long it had been
going on? And I said… Like, I said a few weeks. But I told
her it felt like ages. And I told her about the hamster, and
how I'd almost saved up… I did what you told me to do.
I acted scared. I *showed* how scared I was.

ASHA. Yeah, but what did you *say*?

BETTINA. She started telling the driver he should do
something, and I said… I said what I said to you. That I was
scared they were killing me… And I might have said…
Yeah… I might have said something about them wanting to
hurt me. And *what if* they had a knife? And what if they
followed me off the bus, and the driver and everyone just sat
there doing nothing. Wouldn't they be sorry if something
happened to me then…?

ASHA. You didn't say he actually pulled a knife on you?

Beat.

BETTINA.…It was sort of humiliating, yeah? And she was
being so nice to me, and that made it worse. Made me feel
even more of a loser. Having to admit all that… What
they've been doing… What I've been *letting* them do…
It sounded better… It sort of sounded better, saying there
was a reason for it.

Beat.

It didn't sound so pathetic, I mean. If someone pulls a knife on you, it makes sense you'd be scared and give them your money…

ASHA. So you did say it?

BETTINA. I guess… Yeah… It sort of came out, in the moment. I didn't plan it or anything. I was just remembering what you'd said.

ASHA. I did not tell you to say that.

BETTINA. You told me to act scared. You told me to be pathetic. Loser Bettina, as usual.

ASHA. What are you talking about?

BETTINA. I did what you wanted me to. You said leave it to their imaginations…

ASHA. She must have recognised your uniforms and rung the school.

BETTINA. *I* didn't know she was going to do that, did I?

ASHA. She did the right thing. If it was true.

BETTINA. Am I going to get into trouble…?

ASHA. …I don't know.

BETTINA. Will they tell Mum?

ASHA. …Yeah. Yeah, probably.

BETTINA. Oh shit. What am I going to do?

ASHA. I don't know…

BETTINA. *Asha.*

ASHA. It's Adeel, yeah? No way they're going to buy this shit. Scrawny-ass Adeel with a *blade*? Come on, man. Only an idiot would believe that.

BETTINA. …Right.

ASHA. Just… sit tight and… chill. Okay?

BETTINA. Okay.

Scene Six

The next day, late afternoon. ASHA *sits on the pavement outside the school gates in her uniform, eating a sandwich. She has a black eye.* BETTINA *finds her. She's in her home clothes, jeans, etc.*

BETTINA. Asha?

ASHA. Yep?

BETTINA. What're you doing?

ASHA. What's it look like?

BETTINA. It's getting dark.

ASHA. No shit.

BETTINA. You coming home?

ASHA. Later.

BETTINA (*of her eye*). What happened? Was it Mel Summers again?

ASHA. No.

BETTINA. Does it hurt?

ASHA. …Starting to. Was sort of… numb, at first.

BETTINA. Aren't you supposed to put some ice on it or something? Or like… a steak?

ASHA. Where the hell am I supposed to get a steak?

BETTINA. Shall I ring 999?

ASHA. *No.*

BETTINA. Alright…

ASHA. …I got some frozen peas on it just after it happened. A man in a shop helped me out.

BETTINA. A man in a… shop…? Where?

ASHA. In town.

BETTINA. It happened in town?

ASHA. It's not a big deal. Just don't want to get into aggro with Mum about it.

BETTINA. She's going to notice that, Asha.

ASHA. If I get in after she's gone to work I can get some concealer on it.

BETTINA. Alright… I'll wait with you then.

ASHA. You don't have to.

BETTINA. I don't mind.

> *Beat.* BETTINA *pulls some snacks from her bag. Offers* ASHA *a chocolate bar or some crisps, which* ASHA *accepts. They eat together.*

ASHA (*of the graffiti*). I did this.

BETTINA. Serious?

ASHA. Night I wouldn't accept Mel's apology.

BETTINA. Why?

ASHA. Dunno. Felt like I was putting something right, I suppose.

BETTINA. What's it say?

ASHA. Can't you read?

BETTINA. No offence, Asha. You need to work on your can control.

ASHA. Shut up. What do you know about can control?

BETTINA. Seen loads of TikToks about it. I'll send you some.

ASHA. Hope. It says hope.

BETTINA. Why?

ASHA. Wanted to throw my name up. Like a massive 'fuck you' to Mrs L. But I knew that was stupid and I'd just end up in detention again. So I went with the English translation.

BETTINA. That's so funny.

ASHA. Yeah.

BETTINA. So she's been walking past here for weeks and hasn't clocked it?

ASHA. Suppose so.

BETTINA. She'd never guess it was you, anyway.

ASHA. Maybe not before. Real troublemaker now, aren't I?

BETTINA. Shut up. They don't have troublemakers speaking at the leavers' assembly, do they?

ASHA. Must be why I didn't get a spot.

BETTINA. ...Serious...?

ASHA. Yep.

BETTINA. Why though...?

ASHA. Who cares? It's just a chance for Mr Jeffers to show off and make out we're the best school in the city or something. What a load of bullshit. Want a brown girl on the line-up but not one who might actually say something they don't like.

BETTINA. ...I want a spot when I'm in Year 13.

ASHA. You'll grow out of it.

BETTINA. Who you been fighting with, then?

ASHA. Went for a bubble tea with Rommi in our free period. Adeel was with a couple of his friends outside Games Warehouse.

BETTINA. Who? Lee? Sana?

ASHA. Didn't recognise them.

BETTINA. They did this to you?

ASHA. *No*. They didn't do anything... *I* went over to speak to him.

BETTINA. Why?

ASHA. Wanted to see how he was doing. Say sorry, I guess...

BETTINA. You don't need to say sorry for me.

ASHA. They've suspended him for a *month*, Bettina. It's batshit. Mel Summers punched me in the spine and called me the P-word and all she had to do was push a squeegee around for an hour.

BETTINA.…A month…?

ASHA. While they conduct a 'formal investigation'.

BETTINA. And he lamped you?

ASHA. *No*. He was really shy, actually. But I started trying to explain.

BETTINA. Explain?

ASHA. How what happened was a mistake. How you didn't mean it.

BETTINA *doesn't respond*.

And how we know if he was someone else they wouldn't have reacted the same way.

BETTINA. Do we know that?

ASHA. You think *you'd* have been suspended if someone talked shit about you having a knife?

BETTINA. No, because I'd never do that.

ASHA. Neither did he.

BETTINA. He's given you a black eye though, hasn't he?

ASHA. That wasn't him. His big sister turned up and lost it before I could say anything. Said I was taking the piss.

BETTINA.…There you go, then. He called for back-up.

ASHA. It's not like that, Bettina. Listen.

ASHA *puts her phone on speaker mode and plays a voicemail*.

ADEEL (*voice-over*). 'Hi… Asha… It's me, Adeel… Just wanted to check in with you. Make sure you're okay. Are you? Okay? Look, my sister runs *mad* yeah. I never told her to do that. Believe. I wouldn't. I know things are messed up, but if you want you can bell me. Just want to know you're alright. So… Yeah. It's Adeel, okay? One love.'

Beat.

BETTINA. As if?

ASHA. He wanted to make sure I'm alright.

BETTINA. He's lying, Asha. It's obvious.

ASHA. Why would he do that?

BETTINA. I don't know... So you'll... Tell Mrs L or something. Soften her up while the investigation's still happening.

ASHA. Does not sound like that to me.

BETTINA. Oh you're such an expert?

ASHA. He tried to stop his sister going for me, you know? She threw him down on the pavement – he got hurt as well.

BETTINA. He's probably used to it. They probably spend all their time giving each other slaps. Doesn't mean you have to join in.

ASHA. Will you listen to yourself? You sound like... you sound like Mrs L.

BETTINA. Er, no. I don't think so.

ASHA. You're seeing him through the same eyes. Like he's just this one thing, stuck forever. Running round and round on his little wheel.

BETTINA. Don't compare him to Cardi.

ASHA. How's he supposed to be anything else if no one lets him?

BETTINA. *I'm* not the one stopping him, am I? I'm looking at him through the eyes of someone he's been *robbing* for over two months, and saying exactly what I see. He needed to be taught a lesson. They're not going to pick on me again. They're not going to pick on *anyone*.

ASHA. He's not being investigated for bullying you though, is he? He's being investigated for pulling a *knife*. They're calling him back for a proper interview next week.

BETTINA. ...So he can explain then, can't he?

ASHA. What? That you lied?

BETTINA *shrugs*.

Are they interviewing you too?

BETTINA. Yeah. Mum got a letter.

ASHA. Is she going with you?

BETTINA. Course.

ASHA. What's she said?

BETTINA. Nothing. I mean, she's pissed, isn't she? Thinks they should make an example of him... Are you going to tell her?

ASHA. ...We have to sort this out ourselves.

BETTINA. Why?

ASHA. Because we can't trust Mum on this, alright?

BETTINA. What're you talking about, can't trust her? That's mad.

ASHA. It's not that we can't trust her, okay? I mean, she's more like... she's more like the people on the bus, before you forced them to step up. She's not a bad person, she just won't see why we should do anything about this.

BETTINA. Yeah, well she'd be right. We don't.

Infuriated beat.

ASHA. Mum told me about this girl she grew up with. Mariam. Her best friend. Said growing up they'd get mistaken for one another by the teachers. They'd get called Pakis at school or on the way home. Stuff like that would happen to both of them all the time. *Together*. They just kept their heads down and stayed tight. So it was weird when they started to get treated differently. When Mum started being included in conversations she'd never been in before. Quiet conversations. About something Mariam had said. Or what Mariam had started wearing. And what it meant. How some of the kids started moving away from Mariam in the canteen. Accidentally tripping her up on the playing fields. And some of them started asking Mum weird questions, about whether she was going to convert? And Mum had never really thought much about Mariam being Muslim. It had never seemed any more important than her going to hockey club, or loving Robbie Williams... But all of a sudden it was like it was the biggest thing about her, and Mum couldn't get her head around that.

BETTINA. She said that?

ASHA. Yeah.

BETTINA. Well, what're you telling me for…?

ASHA. You get it'll be worse for Adeel than it would be for one of us, right?

BETTINA. Not necessarily…

ASHA. They're treating him like he's some sort of serious threat, yeah? Why is skinny-ass Adeel a threat? Because he's not just a kid with a knife, he's a brown kid with a knife. He's a Muslim brown kid with a knife.

BETTINA. But he didn't have a knife.

ASHA. *Exactly.* You know they could exclude him for this? Right before his GCSEs. This could ruin his life.

BETTINA. He was going to flunk them anyway.

ASHA. Shut up, Bettina. You don't know that. Mum lied to me about Mariam. Tried to make out everything's fine now. That Mariam sorted herself out and got this amazing career at this shit-hot uni. But I looked it up. There's no Mariam at King's.

BETTINA. So maybe she got the name of the place wrong. Or, or… maybe Mariam's changed her name.

ASHA. I don't think so, Bettina. Mum was bare shifty when she was telling me, and I spent two hours on Google trying to find something, anything.

BETTINA. Why would she lie?

ASHA. I don't know, because she's embarrassed? Ashamed? Maybe she was a shit friend, and she let Mariam down. And in a way, she let herself down too.

BETTINA. It wasn't her giving Mariam a hard time, was it?

ASHA. No, but I reckon Mum realised she didn't have to put up with it. She wasn't a Muslim. She had a way out. Not an easy one, but it was there, if she was ready to take it.

BETTINA. You don't know that.

ASHA. How else do you explain how shifty she's being?

BETTINA. I don't know, but it's not the same thing. So you can stop trying to guilt-trip me because it won't work.

ASHA. They've told him to write an essay about second chances while he's suspended.

BETTINA. How do you know?

ASHA. I called him back.

BETTINA. What…?

ASHA. I think it's just to keep him busy, but if he does a decent job it could make a difference. Said I'd help him with it.

BETTINA. You serious?

ASHA. If he can just make Mrs L see she's got him wrong, look at him differently, maybe she'll treat him better when he has to go in.

BETTINA. So you're going to… you're going to waste bare hours writing an essay for *Adeel*?

ASHA. I'm just giving him a bit of help.

BETTINA. That means writing it for him, Asha. He's thick as shit, everyone knows that.

ASHA. Don't say that.

BETTINA. Why not?

ASHA. Because it's not true. And also you shouldn't talk about people like that.

BETTINA. You know what they used to call me?

ASHA. It's not the same, Bettina…

BETTINA. Plan B. They called me Plan B. As in the morning-after pill? They said I was like emergency contraception. They said I'm so gross you just have to think of me and you won't want to bone any more.

ASHA. That's shit. I'm sorry.

BETTINA. But you're still going to help him…?

ASHA. If it was you… If something like this happened to you, I'd want someone to, like, give you some support…

BETTINA. How can you say that? I had to *beg* you to help me. I had to get down on my *knees*, and even then you wouldn't step up. Not really. But Adeel just has to drop you one whiny voicenote and you come running.

ASHA. I know it must seem like that, but / [it's not the same]

BETTINA. It seems like that because it *is* like that, Asha. Just like Adeel really is a bare loser, whatever angle you look at him. Mum was right, you know? You just get a kick out of winding people up. Making yourself look all big. Like you're some sort of... maverick or something. Slagging off Gandhi to Mrs L.

ASHA. That's not what I did.

BETTINA. Yes it is. And now you're stabbing me in the back too.

ASHA. I'm not, Bettina. I'd never do that.

BETTINA *grabs her bag.*

BETTINA. So *don't.*

BETTINA *exits with fury.* ASHA *is shaken. She takes out her phone, and her Bluetooth speaker. She plays the recordings of Ambedkar and Pankhurst's audio biography. It's almost as if they're talking to each other. Almost as if they're talking to her.*

AMBEDKAR (*voice-over*). 'Public conscience means conscience which becomes agitated at every wrong, no matter who is the sufferer, and it means that everybody, whether he suffers that particular wrong or not, is prepared to join him in order to get him relieved.'

NARRATOR (*voice-over*). '...where we shall all be brothers and sisters, where everyone will have enough.'

Scene Seven

Later that night. ASHA *waits at the bus stop, alone. It's getting dark.*

ASHA (*direct address*). I've been searching and searching online to hear Sylvia. Like, you can read loads of her speeches on the internet, and there's PDFs and audiobooks of stuff about her and everything, but you can't hear her reading them. The only place you can hear her voice is this broadcast where she's talking about her mum.

SYLVIA (*voice-over*). 'My mother Emmeline Pankhurst had the most vital gift of all, that the cause for which she was fighting was the most vital of all the causes.'

ASHA (*direct address*). Her voice is deeper than I thought it would be. But she doesn't sound angry or anything. The whole thing is about her mum, and the work she did, and she doesn't talk about how they fell out, or how Emmeline and Christabel dragged her in the papers. And I've listened to it, again and again. Trying to work out if there's something underneath there, in between the lines, to hint at what happened between them. But there isn't…

SYLVIA (*voice-over*). 'This strong conviction, with her beautiful speaking voice, and ability to impress her ideas in words all classes of people could understand, gave her great power to influence others.'

ASHA *plays the voicenote she recorded earlier to herself.*

ASHA (*voice-over*). 'Humans are mortal. So are ideas. An idea needs propagation as much as a plant needs watering. Otherwise both will wither and die.'

(*Direct address*). I've been thinking about what my ideas are. *My* convictions. Not what will get me eighty-five per cent from Mrs L, or in my exams. Or… make Mum happy. I've been trying to work out why what I think gets me in so much shit.

She plays the voicenote again.

(*Voice-over.*) '…otherwise both will wither and die.'

(*Direct address.*) So I try to talk to Mum again. I take Ambedkar and Sylvia with me. For back-up. I tell her I know she's a liar. I hurt inside when she tries to argue. I ask her for the name of the university again. She pretends she can't remember. I show her the website, the place she told me about. The place where Mariam should be, on the staff page, smiling out alongside everyone else. She goes quiet. I wonder what she's going to lie about now. I realise she's crying. I've never seen her cry before. I don't know what to say. So I just blurt out, maybe if Gandhi really saw Dalits as equal he wouldn't have fought so hard against Ambedkar? And maybe if Emmeline and Christabel saw no difference between them and women workers they wouldn't have pushed for their brothers and their sons to go fight in the war?

And then I play her those quotes. Partly because I want to hear them again, but also because it's easier than finding any more of my own words… And she stops crying. And we both listen. And for ages neither of us say anything. And she tells me she's been reading up on Ambedkar. And she tells me how proud she is of me, and she never says shit like that and now I'm trying not to cry. She tries to explain she might have been born and raised here, and never known anything different, but there's always been an edge to it. She's always been made to feel she doesn't belong, not properly. And how Gandhiji, and temple and everything feel like a route back home for her. A lifeline. A life*boat*. And at first it felt like I'd put a great big puncture in it. But how I'd made her stop and think, and remember…

And she tells me, and now she's speaking so quiet I can barely hear her, and I have to stand right up close, and I can smell her perfume, and I can feel her breath on me, and for a minute it feels like I'm little again. And she tells me Mariam came into school one day wearing hijab. And how, looking back, Mum could see how brave that was. But at the time, loads of kids ripped the piss out of Mariam. And some of them were their friends. Her friends. And Mum was sort of… embarrassed. And Mariam ignored them, and when a couple of kids tried to pull it off in the playground, she just walked quicker. But the same kids stopped Mum. And one of them had taken off his jumper and was wearing it on his head like an idiot. And it was stupid, but everyone was laughing, and they wouldn't let Mum get past. And she was scared, but she knew she was supposed to laugh along, so she made herself. And they told her she wasn't like the others and she knew what that meant. And they asked her if Mariam was a terrorist. And it was a new word but they'd all learned what it meant really quickly. And they said if anyone could vouch for Mariam, it would be Mum. And Mum wanted to back her up. She so badly wanted to. But she started thinking about what this would mean for her, if things got worse with Mariam in a few days, or a few weeks, and she hesitated long enough for everyone to understand. Long enough for Mariam's face to fall and for Mum to feel her complete sense of betrayal. And I know I should be angry, or disappointed, or something. But I just feel numb. I don't want to hear any more talk. I want to know what Mum's going to do about it, what *we're* going to do. Because we do need a lifeline. But we need to build it for one another here and now, don't we?

Scene Eight

Two weeks later. ASHA *joins* BETTINA *in the bedroom they share.* BETTINA *is setting up Cardi's cage. Cardi's in a cardboard box beside her.* BETTINA *wears a different school uniform.*

ASHA (*pulling some packets from her rucksack*). Got these for Cardi.

BETTINA. What are they?

ASHA. Hamster snacks.

BETTINA. Thought she wasn't a hamster?

ASHA (*reading one of the packets*). They're a 'delicious milky treat for small mammals'. The woman in the pet shop said her capybara goes crazy for them.

BETTINA. Right…

ASHA. Got her strawberry and mango ones.

BETTINA.... Okay, thanks

Beat.

That it?

ASHA. Got something for you too.

BETTINA. What?

ASHA. Just hear me out before you say anything, okay?

BETTINA. Why?

ASHA. I've got something to read to you. From Adeel. It's something from Adeel.

BETTINA *starts to put Cardi away, making to leave.*

I get it, yeah? But it'll only take two minutes. Please, Bettina?

BETTINA.... Two minutes, then I'm meeting some friends.

ASHA. That's great. From Gateway?

BETTINA. Yeah.

ASHA. Barely been two weeks and you're making friends?

BETTINA. You don't have to sound so surprised.

ASHA. I'm not. I'm just saying... That's good. I'm pleased for you...

BETTINA. How long's this going to take?

ASHA. Alright, I'll just read it...

BETTINA *pauses, but is unable to look at* ASHA. ASHA *reads aloud from her phone.*

'They keep talking about this thing called a "second chance".
They keep telling me I can have one, just one. Second
chance. I'm not sure what I have to do to get it though.
I think they know what it is I'm supposed to be doing.
To deserve it. But they won't spell it out and I'm not clever
enough to work it out for myself. Maybe I'm not clever
enough to have a second chance.

Like, I want them to see my potential, but I don't know what
that is, and I'm scared of saying the wrong thing. So mainly
I don't say anything. And I know that makes them angry, but
that makes me want to say even less. And I know I'm not
doing the right thing. I know I'm messing up this second
chance.

Thing is, I think maybe I've worked it out. Why it feels all
wrong. Maybe I don't know the right thing to say because
I'm talking to the wrong person...? It's not up to Mrs L,
or Mr Jeffers, or any of them to give me a second chance.
I never took their money, or hassled them on the bus, or said
shitty things to them. I never pretended not to notice they
were crying.

A friend told me we only get two billion heartbeats. Two
billion beats, and then we die. Every time I'm scared to
speak because I might get into trouble. Every time I'm
scared to act because I'll get it wrong. Every time I just act
the way I think they want me to. That's eating into my two
billion beats. I don't want to waste any more of them doing
that. I just want to say sorry. To the right person. To Bettina.
I just want her to know I'm sorry. That's all. And that's it,
really. I don't have anything else to say.'

Beat.

BETTINA. You told him about the two billion beats? ...Why
would you do that?

ASHA. I wanted him to understand what they'd done to you.
He needs to know how scared they made you feel.

BETTINA. Why? So he can keep laughing at me while he's
suspended? Do I ever get to stop being poor, pathetic
Bettina, for fuck's sake...?

ASHA. You're not, it's not like that.

BETTINA. What is it like, then?

ASHA. How's he supposed to change, how's he supposed to
feel sorry, properly feel sorry, if he doesn't get how he hurt
you? I just wanted him to know. He *should* know.

Beat.

BETTINA. Yeah, well good work. Mrs L'll love it.

ASHA. It's not for Mrs L. It's not for his formal interview. It's not for any of that.

BETTINA....He didn't write that by himself.

ASHA. I didn't write it, I just helped him get it down.

BETTINA. As if.

ASHA. He told me not to show it to anyone else. He said it was only for you.

Beat.

BETTINA. I don't have to accept his apology.

ASHA. Yeah, okay, fair enough. But your interview's at the school today, right? You can tell the truth to Mrs L. You can end this.

BETTINA....So Mum can be pissed with me, instead?

ASHA. I don't think so, I think she'll get it.

BETTINA. Oh, so now we can trust her?

ASHA. She went to speak to Mrs L. She's got her to give me a spot at the assembly at De Montfort. Backed me up about the unconscious bias stuff. Got a feeling she didn't hold back.

BETTINA. Good. You should have a spot.

ASHA. I want Adeel to have it.

BETTINA....Why? (*Of Adeel's apology.*) So he can read that out and everyone'll think he's the good guy?

ASHA. He won't read this out – it's just for you.

BETTINA. You've worked your arse off for this. You deserve it.

ASHA. Doesn't mean anything to me any more.

BETTINA. You can put it on your UCAS, can't you? They only pick three kids, three kids every year. No way Adeel should be one of them. After everything he's done? No way.

ASHA. It could turn things around for him. It's just another ticked box for me.

BETTINA. Fuck's sake, Asha, you get a black eye for him, you help him write an essay, now you want to give him your spot?

ASHA. He *can* speak for himself. If he's given a chance.

BETTINA. It's like you're in love with the guy.

ASHA. Barely spoken to him since you two were little kids.

BETTINA. So why're you doing all this shit for him, then?

ASHA.…No one's ever listened to him.

BETTINA. Whose idea is this? Does he even want to do it? Does he even have anything he wants to say?

ASHA.…Yeah. Of course he does.

Beat.

BETTINA. Yeah, well he's not allowed on school premises. And that'll include the leavers' assembly.

ASHA. They'll let him if you tell the truth.

Beat.

BETTINA. All I wanted was a fresh start.

ASHA. Yeah. But Adeel deserves one too. Right?

BETTINA *busies herself sorting out Cardi's cage, inscrutable.*

It's your choice. But you could do something amazing this afternoon. Something brave. If you wanted to.

ASHA *exits.* BETTINA *watches Cardi for a few moments. Conflicted beat. She gets together her jacket and bag and exits.*

Scene Nine

ASHA *prepares for the school leavers' assembly backstage at De Montfort Hall, nervously running through a stack of note cards, practising her lines quietly to herself and trying to memorise them.*

ADEEL (*voice-over*). 'Hi. Asha. It's Adeel. Yeah. Thanks for your message. I appreciate it. Big time. But, look, man… I don't know if I can do that, you get me? They been getting us to read out our work at the PRU and that's only like five people but I still mess it up. I don't want to piss off Jeffers. You're out of here but I still got Year 13 to go, you get me? I don't know if the leavers' assembly is for me, yeah?'

ASHA (*voice-over*). Hey Adeel. Sorry I missed you. Yeah, course I get it. I don't want you to get in trouble, but that's the whole point, right? They think they can just quietly let you back in like nothing happened. Why? So *they* can save face? That's not right. You said you're scared of saying the wrong thing, but I don't think it's about that. I think Jeffers and Mrs L and… everyone… they need to *listen*. Learn to listen, if that's what it takes. It's up to you but I really think you should do this. I'll hold your spot, okay?

ASHA *walks onstage, into the spotlight.*

(*Direct address.*) Hello, everyone. Sorry. I knew I'd be nervous so I made some notes…

ASHA *takes out some note cards from her pocket.*

I spent a long time thinking what to say. First draft, I put in a load of quotes from people I've been reading about. People I admire. It felt like it carried more weight. Felt like they had it all worked out so it was best to just listen to what they had to say. But I edited a bit of them out with each draft, until I realised I wasn't going to use any of those quotes. I have to say this in my own words. We'll never be together like this again. But it's not like a full stop, it's more like a dot-dot-dot, because we don't know what's going to happen next. And maybe we don't feel like we have much say over that dot-dot-dot. And I know the more you feel like that, the smaller you feel too. And it makes you do and say stuff you know is wrong, just to protect yourself from what might happen, what *could* happen. You might even make up things to cover your back. I just... I guess there're a lot of things that stop us saying what we really think. Or... doing things we really believe in. To make the world how we think it should be. How we want it to be, I mean. I used to think it was cowardice, but now I think everyone gets scared sometimes. It's what we do in the face of it that counts. And I'm starting to think we make out it's much more complicated than it really is. I'm starting to think maybe it can be simple.

You see, I've been learning about suffragettes who saw demanding votes for women as just the beginning. And Indian independence fighters who wanted caste equality to be just the start. But we don't know so much about them, do we? Because what they were asking for meant turning the world upside down, and some people couldn't handle that. So even now we have this idea of who was 'the right kind of suffragette' and who was the 'right kind of freedom fighter'.

She scans the audience, searching for someone. She realises Adeel has entered the hall, and smiles.

What I'm trying to say is, I know maybe some of you think I'm the right kind of kid to have this spot. But I don't want it, unless I can share it.

The spotlight grows around her as she holds out the mic to Adeel.

Blackout.

AMBEDKAR (*voice-over*). 'I can ask the political-minded Hindus, "Are you fit for political power even though you do not allow a large class of your own countrymen like the untouchables to use public schools? Are you fit for political power even though you do not allow them the use of public wells? Are you fit for political power even though you do not allow them the use of public streets? Are you fit for political power even though you do not allow them to wear what apparel or ornaments they like? Are you fit for political power even though you do not allow them to eat any food they like?" I can ask a string of such questions. But these will suffice...'

Lights slowly dim.

www.nickhernbooks.co.uk

facebook.com/nickhernbooks

twitter.com/nickhernbooks